Beneath the Bonsai Tree

A Small Book of Poems

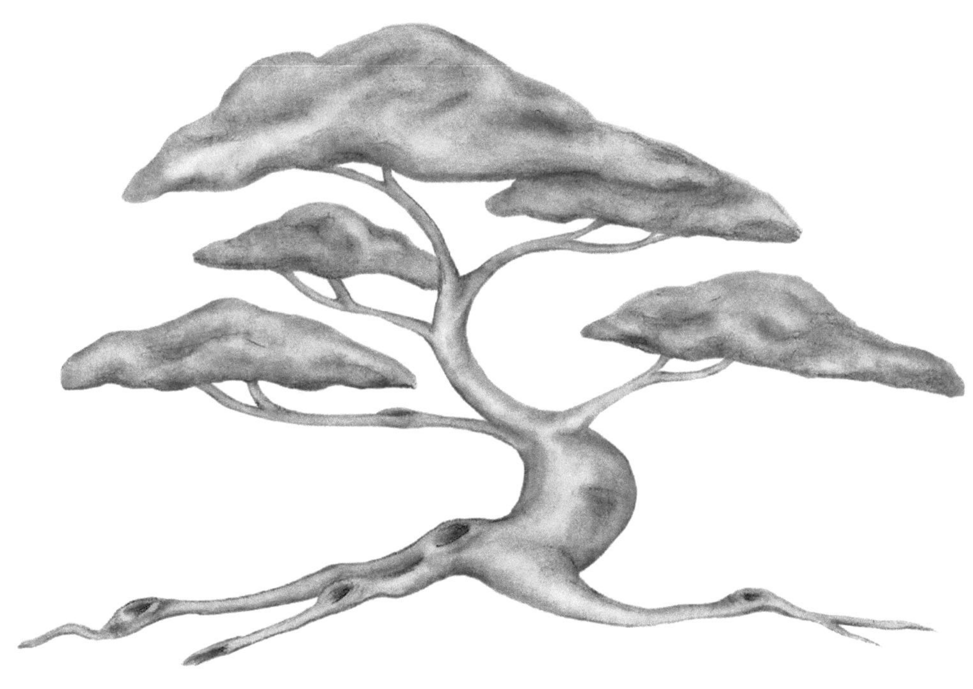

Self-published with
IngramSpark®

Written and Illustrated by G. Lubbers

Dedicated to Zachary, Thomas, Victoria, and Peter

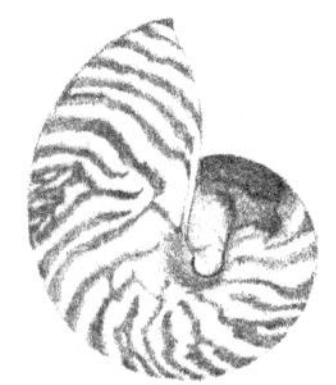

List of Poems

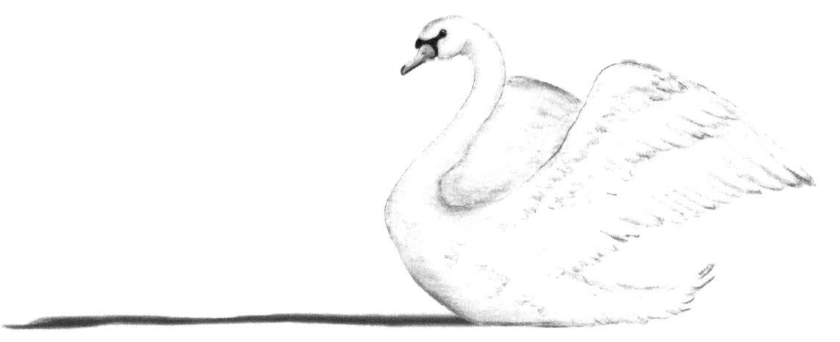

Beneath the Bonsai Tree

Beneath the bonsai tree,
Where the painted ponies roam free,
Lie meadows of grasses, and fields so green,
Flowers full of colorful blooms,
All found abundantly,
Beneath the bonsai tree.

Stretching its limbs under billowy clouds,
Its leaves trimmed preen and pristine;
We found our hearts filled with sweet wonder,
Searching for peace and serenity.

Grace takes the stage
As a pair of hearts that whisper,
The swans glide as on mirrored glass.
In quiet elegance they move along,
Perfectly, in their dance.

Look to the east
Where the egret flies,
The bluebirds' orchestra fills the sky,
And we'll walk beyond
The dandelion path
That leads us to the lakeside.

Sweet honeysuckle fills pockets of air
As the hummingbirds flitter and flutter.
Though they grant no one else a care
As they fuss over the sweet, red clover.

As we made our way down
You were humming a song
When the mockingbird laughed out loud.
A repetitious phrase we did not know,
And yet we still sang along.

A silly tune without many words
The notes both low, and high;
It was fun as we laughed,
But we must have hit a nerve,
He left without saying goodbye.

We ran for shelter late in the day,
As the raindrops cooled our skin,
Cleansing us from yesterday's tolls.
Finding refuge,
We stood quite still,
The gentle silence feeding our souls.

The yellows and reds slipped into slumber
Hinting the end of the day.
Walking back the pebbled path,
We met our graceful friends again,
As the daylight melted away.

The stars raised a blanket to cover the night,
Seemingly to sparkle with delight,
Leaving us feeling fully grateful,
With the simple gift of harmony,
Found under the caring boughs,
Beneath the bonsai tree.

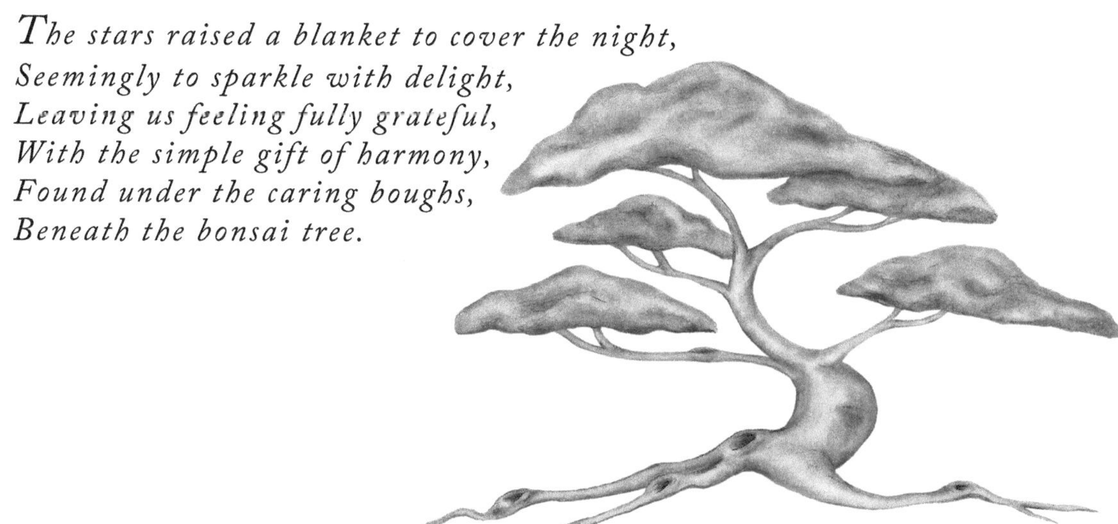

Opened Doors

Because of you,
I have begun to live,
And walk about the stars
With all their rolling promises.

I have begun to breathe,
To smell the lilac's sweet perfume,
As if spring were never-ending.

I danced with creatures below the sea,
And listened to their names;
Beautiful as the wind called to me,
Silent whispers unlocking chains.

One life that grows to grasp the vine,
And reap all of its riches.
Open-mouthed to drink the wine,
And kiss the rain petals
Softly lighted up by drops of hope.

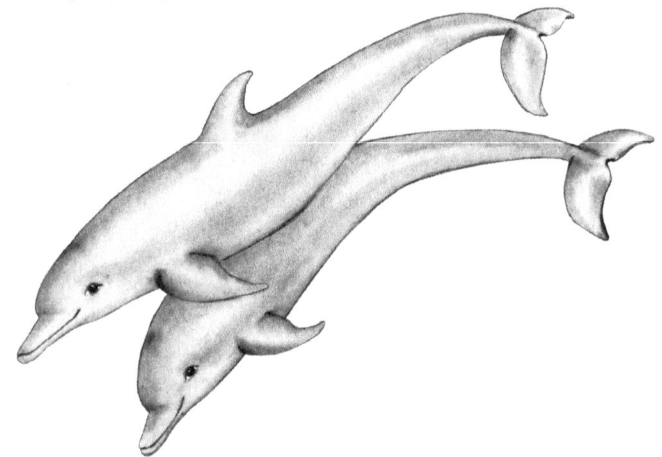

A Night of Tribulation

At night is when I touch you;
Naked, face to face
Reaching out to wonderland,
Beyond the safe embrace.

The numbers flying by,
Barely escape the grin,
Worn by a stealth cat
Who knows you can never win.

A game, which only the queen commands,
She took your dreams into forbidden lands.
A strange world not too far from here,
It comes in view only when you're near.

A fantasy
That could never come to be;
You're real, all right,
But only real to me.

And when the moon casts shadows,
I see only two,
In one framed mirror,
Me and you.

A haunting story,
Which replays itself
In a fairy-tale book
That never leaves the shelf.

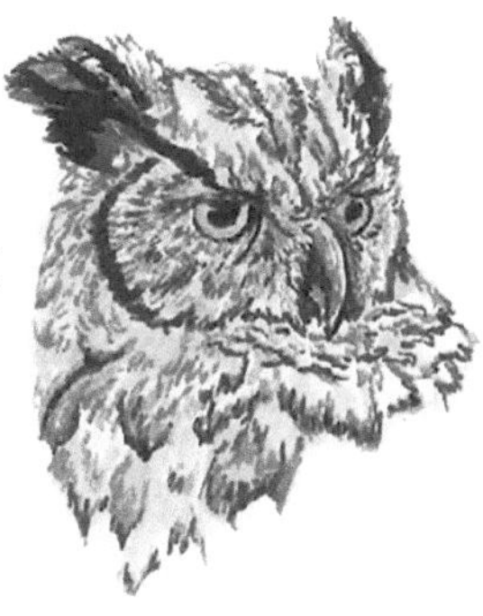

Little Mustard Seed

Oh, little mustard seed
What gift could you give to me?
With promises that slip through my grasp,
Searching for some state of peace,
Is all I truly ask.

As I hold you in the palm of my hand,
You're nothing but a grain of sand.
Why am I unable to understand
The power that you command?

Internal struggles are proudly owned,
Yet no one seems to mind.
The storms are so quiet to withhold,
Not one of them is kind.

With haunting doubts that linger inside,
Stripping my every sense of pride.
A daunting task I chose to climb,
That stone, cold mountain of time.

Swirling, storm clouds hide its peak,
But trepidation is quite consoling.
Fear disguised as a comforting friend,
A slippery slope that does not end.

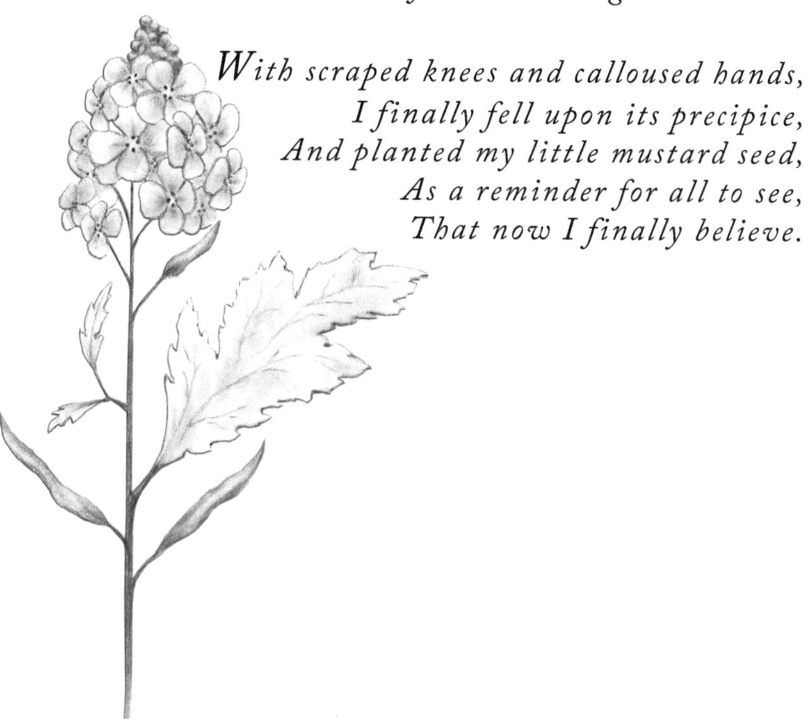

The mountain shuddered while it laughed,
Dragging me down its icy slope,
My feet feeling as if shattered by glass,
Breaking my every sense of hope.

Its laughter was quite ominous,
Acquainted with my pain.
With thunderous waves
Of daunting clouds,
All of my efforts were in vain.

And yet you kept your silence,
No movement to remark.
Alone, in deafening quiet,
You left me standing in the dark.

With scraped knees and calloused hands,
I finally fell upon its precipice,
And planted my little mustard seed,
As a reminder for all to see,
That now I finally believe.

Be Kind

Tomorrow will be a brighter day.
Tomorrow we will laugh and play.

We'll offer each other a helping hand.
With love and care, and a willingness to understand.

Take a deep breath, and reach for your dreams.
There is nothing you can't do if you just believe.

Just as the flowers we planted need nurture and care;
A simple gesture that we can all share.

With a tender touch we can help them to grow,
Along with two simple words that we should all know.

A beautiful thought to keep in mind,
Always remember to just Be Kind.

Wishful

If I could sit here quietly,
And touch the stars above.
If I could kiss each raindrop,
Sent from the heavens with love.

If I could count each grain of sand,
Reaching far across the lands.
If I could capture the sun's light,
And hold it in the palm of my hand.

I would carry your burden.
I would carry your spear.
I would fight your battles,
So you would never fear.

Love is greater than any word,
Greater than a mountain's roar;
Just knowing that you're near,
My heart truly soars.

And though tomorrow may bring sorrow,
Know that others will bring sheer delight.
I pray that each hope is promised,
And that the angels keep you in their sight.

At times I lay in troubled sleep,
Yet for my own life to be complete,
What I wish for with all my heart,
Is for you to live in peace.

Mother Earth

Sometimes I sit and wonder,
Of what tomorrow will bring,
Watching the billowy clouds float by
As I hear a mockingbird sing.

The cherry blossoms awoke overnight,
Their beauty bringing me to tears;
Each petal greeting the sun's light,
Their fragrance feeding every appetite.

Beneath a sky of a million stars
The giant red forest sleeps.
Keeping a watchful eye,
Offering sanctuary,
Every creature is at peace.

The subject seems to be quite mute
As simple gifts are feared to fade;
Both judge and jury can be jaded,
Lost intentions along the way.

And while the clock stands guard,
It still keeps perfect measure.
Standing stoic from our past,
Losing sight of their future,
We guaranteed our own pleasures.

The storms at times
Can be wild and chaotic,
As lightning lights up the sky;
Though not in anger,
From pain, they reel,
As if they were to cry.

Red and amber hues remark of faded days
As memories replay the deepest desires we seek.
Yet everywhere that we can see
Is the heart and soul of life that sings.

As the Milky Way drips onto the ocean's waves
Graceful dancers sing below.
With a whisper at first,
They call you by name,
Though you may never know.

They have a pleading message,
Though it's kept in quiet form,
Barely able to be heard,
They simply whisper,
"Please take care of our Mother Earth."

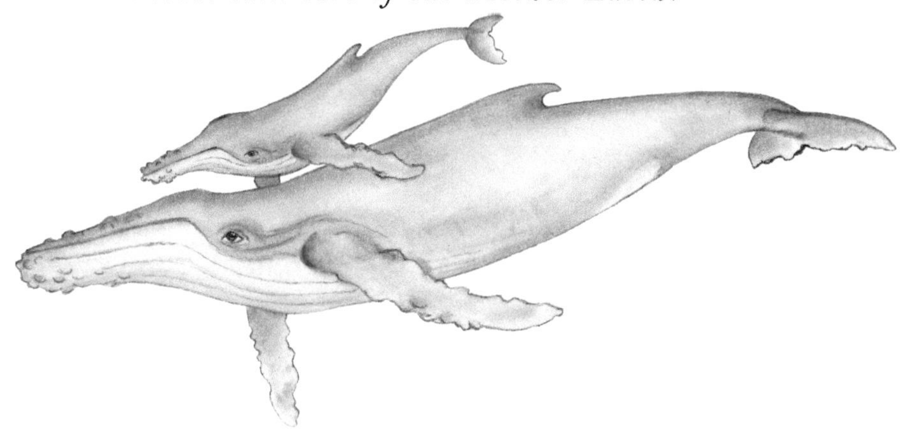

Just Breathe

just breathe
and count to ten,
just be calm
and rely on your zen.

don't look past tomorrow
forget yesterday,
though the world's quickly turning,
it's all going to be okay.

through all of life's turmoils,
through life's ups and downs,
through the troubled waters,
we'll all get around.

life's bumpy roads
never promised to be smooth,
but we'll walk hand in hand
with nothing left to prove.

as long as we have each other
we'll get through each toll,
with faith, hope, and love,
to rise above it all.

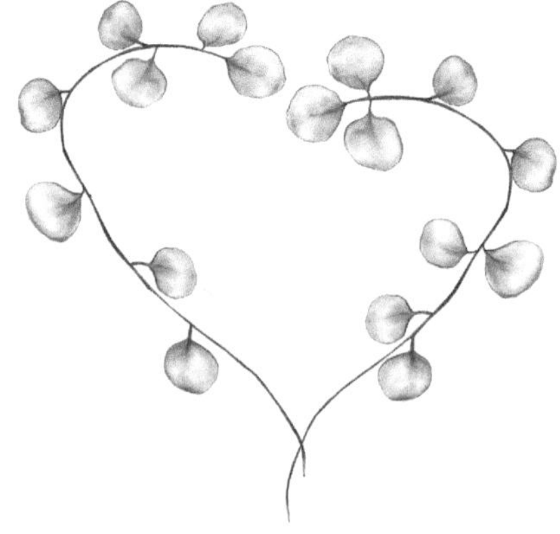

The Sun Rises

I too have seen dark days,
Wishing for brighter tomorrows.
Wanting nothing more than to escape,
Fierce and turbulent storms.

The grasses are greener after the rains,
The flowers are in full bloom,
The sun shines lightly, warming our skin,
The stars dance behind the moon.

Though after the winds fade away,
The clouds may still seem dark,
Causing you to feel a little lost,
Fearing the pain will never end.

Know that the sun will rise again,
Never again will you travel alone,
Because you and I
Will walk that path,
Hand in hand,
Together, my friend.

My Friend, Time

Oh time,
Why can't you be a friend of mine?
Just as I close my eyes for bed,
The unwanted buzzing
Seeps through my head.

Where do you hide when the moon is out?
With my emotions you just play about.
Reruns of my entire day,
And matters of tomorrow,
I continue to chase.

Like a storm with rains and heavy thunder,
You linger all night long.
As I lay still in false slumber,
With mean efforts to correct all my wrongs.

You're not very kind,
Though I've asked quite politely.
You're very proud of your job.
You never take it too lightly.

The sounds of the clock
Can be haunting at times,
Each second and minute they creep,
Stretching out for miles,
Teasing me,
Taunting me,
Digging in so deep.

When at work you seem to stand so still,
Moving at an absurd, steady pace.
But then you laugh at my leisure,
Twisting the precious minutes,
Turning them into your race.

Each day has the same counted seconds,
Measured with equal grains of sand.
Just one more hour is needed,
So why can't you just understand?

And now that my yesterday is washed away
With the glowing hues of the sunrise.
The new morning acts with haste,
Despite my heavy, heeded sighs.

Quietly, I whisper,
To my good, ole friend time;
A longing plead,
A simple task,
Just five more minutes,
Is that too much to ask?

Assurance

Again I'll laugh, and yes, I'll cry,
And I'll be strong inside.
Walking away from a long-ago time,
And saying my own goodbyes.

Expressions of my inner self
Have greatly been subdued.
Thrown away with the costume of life,
A life I chose not to pursue.

Misunderstood silence heard from above
As prayers of sorrow grow with fatigue.
Hiding in the twilight at times we fear
The reality we choose to believe.

For our tomorrows are yet to be born,
And the sunrise will soon be forgotten.
The storms from the past swiftly roll in,
Riding on hearts that are easily broken.

But we still set our sails to race past the horizon,
Comfortably knowing that the sun may not rise,
And the moon could not shine,
But with your hand in mine,
Our hearts will never divide.

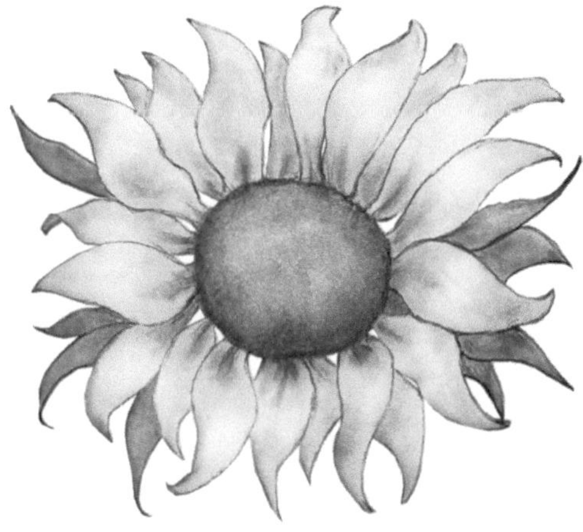

I Will

With Love,
 I will learn to Walk.
With Laughter,
 I will learn to Sing.
With Peace,
 I will learn to Give.
With Hope,
 I will learn to Live.

www.ingramcontent.com/pod-product-compliance
Lightning Source LLC
Chambersburg PA
CBHW042146030726
47599CB00002B/631